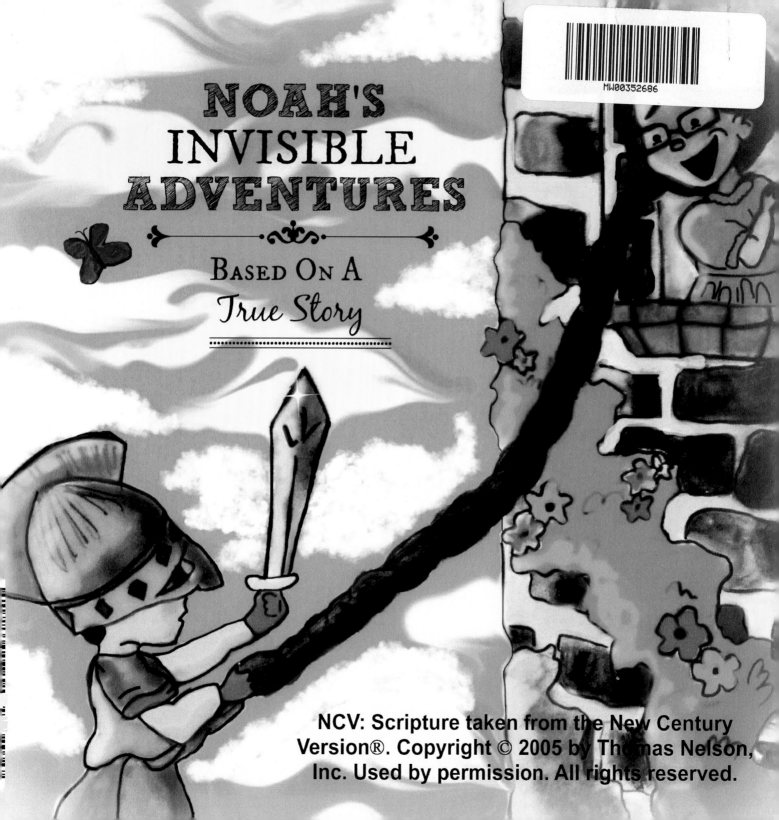

NOAH'S INVISIBLE ADVENTURES

Based On A
True Story

For Jesus...

Immortal, Invisible, King, Best Friend, and Author of EVERY real adventure.

For Noah...

You never cease to amaze me little buddy! Thank you for taking me on your adventures and for showing me what Jesus looks like!

Treasure Hunt

INSTRUCTIONS

AHOY, ye maties and fellow journeyers into this here BLAST of a book! Before ye set to sailing this wild sea of words,

there's something ye NEED TO KNOW if ye want to find the **treasure!!!**

Hidden inside these pages is a trail of

 SHINY STARS

That will lead ye straight to the loot!

All ye needs do is FIND the stars, then MATCH their COLORS and page numbers to the chest awaitin ye in the BACK OF THE BOOK.

Tis a treasure worth more than ALL the gold in the world, to be sure!

The journey may be long, but stay the course me hearties!

ME THINKS YOU WON'T BE SORRY! :)

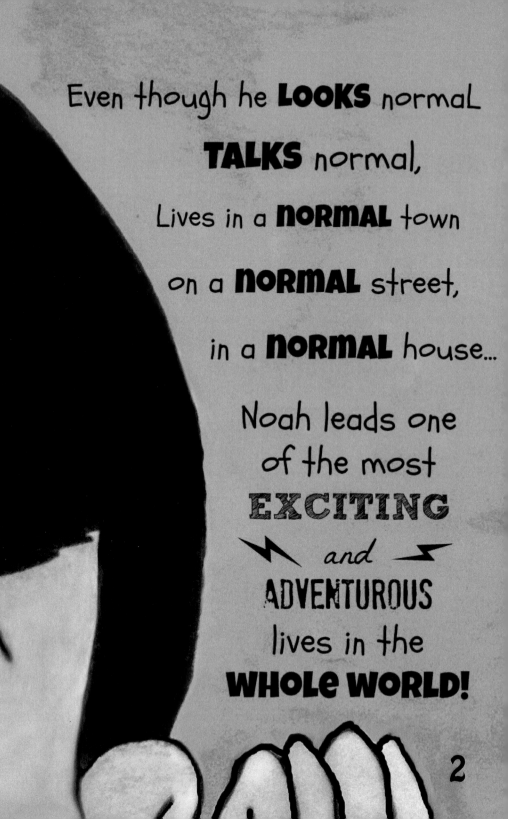

Even though he **LOOKS** normal

TALKS normal,

Lives in a **NORMAL** town

on a **NORMAL** street,

in a **NORMAL** house...

Noah leads one of the most **EXCITING** and **ADVENTUROUS** lives in the **WHOLE WORLD!**

2

OR EATING

entire buckets

OF CHEESEBALLS

BY

HIMSELF!

NOM! NOM!

YUM! YUM!

(OK, SO MAYBE THE CHEESEBALL THING ISN'T THAT NORMAL, BUT YOU GET THE PICTURE...)

UGHHHHHHH...

So just WHERE is all the excitement!?

You won't find the answer in what you CAN see, but in what you CAN'T see!

Noah isn't extraordinary because of what happens on the OUTSIDE of him, but because of what happens on the INSIDE of him.

NOAH'S BRAIN

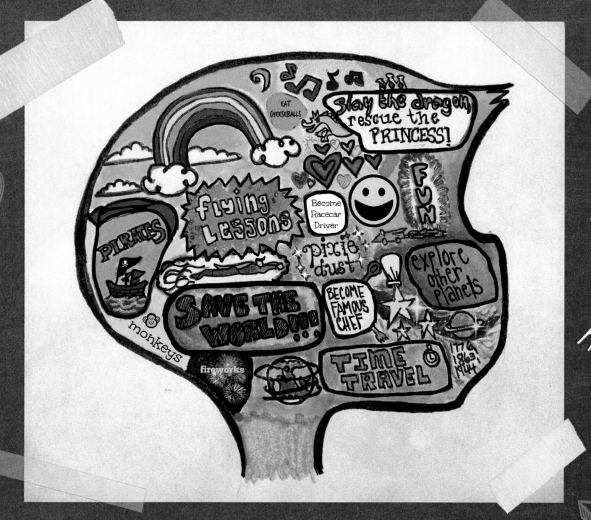

The invisible parts of a person are always what matter most. This is especially true in Noah's case for one VERY important reason...

NOAH IS BLIND.

This means that Noah's eyes don't work like our eyes do. When we look at this picture, we see

 **COLORS** and **TREES,**

and *brightly decorated flowers,*

SNOW CAPPED MOUNTAINS,

SPARKLING LAKES,

and

 cute, fluffy animals

 When Noah looks at this same picture...

→

9

He sees THIS.

NOTHING.

A blank page.

To get a better idea of what Noah's world is like, close your eyes and cover them with your hands.

THIS IS WHAT NOAH SEES, ALL DAY, EVERY DAY!

"WHERE IS THE ADVENTURE IN THAT!?" you may ask.

How can he go on adventures when he can't see anything?!

What you didn't know is that Noah has a special set of HIDDEN EYES that let him look at the world.

(We have them too, we just don't use them as much as Noah does.)

These hidden eyes are called the **"EYES OF YOUR IMAGINATION."**

We open these eyes when we pretend SOMETHING IS REAL, and bring it to life in our minds.

YOURSELF AS A

SUPERHERO

SOARING THROUGH THE NIGHT
TO RESCUE A CITY
IN DANGER!!!

UP! UP!
and
AWAY!

Or as a brave explorer
CIRCLING THE PLANET
IN A BUCKET
LIFTED BY HUNDREDS
of bright balloons!

And if you're feeling especially creative
YOU COULD BE A FLUFF-TAILED RABBIT
being chased by a snaggle- toothed
FOX!

20

Since Noah cannot use his normal eyes, he has to use the eyes of his IMAGINATION ALL THE TIME!

This means that **Noah's life is** ONE GIANT INVISIBLE ADVENTURE!

22

What **we** see Noah doing **IS COMPLETELY DIFFERENT** FROM WHAT NOAH sees himself doing!

23

When we see
NOAH
swinging
from his
PLAYSET.

NOAH SEES HIMSELF swinging from TREE to TREE LIKE A WILD JUNGLE BOY!

NOAH SEES HIMSELF
SOARING THROUGH
the SKIES
HIGH ABOVE THE EARTH.

(HE THINKS THE CLOUDS
TASTE LIKE COTTON CANDY.)

(NOTE: Do not eat soap. It does NOT taste like cotton candy.)

WHEN WE SEE NOAH taking his bath COVERED IN BUBBLES & SLIPPERY SOAP...

Noah sees himself **BATTLING THE NASTY,** Neverland Pirates!!

HE IS
CHASED
BY A
HUNGRY
CROCODILE!

34

When we see Noah climbing the stairs to catch his big sister....

Noah isn't done surprising us yet!

HE HAS ANOTHER SET OF HIDDEN EYES CALLED THE,

EYES OF FAITH!

We open our faith eyes when we believe what God says, EVEN when we can't see it coming true.

FAITH IS THE MOST IMPORTANT thing we could have!

It is the key that unlocks the door to our hearts, so that Jesus **CAN COME IN!** KNOWING JESUS is the **GREATEST ADVENTURE** IN THE WHOLE WORLD!

38

He practices faith
when he trusts his family
to give him food
and water that
is safe to eat and drink

**If Noah decided
to trust himself**
instead of his family,
HE MIGHT END UP IN SERIOUS DANGER!
**He might just cook the
FAMILY CAT!**

In the same way, we are only safe when
we learn to trust God instead of ourselves.

So when Noah heard that God had made the world as a perfect place where people could get to KNOW and LOVE God, Noah was EXCITED!

When Noah heard that the world had turned it's back on God, and that our mistakes had separated us from Him, Noah was SO SAD.

(WE CALL THIS SEPARATION, DEATH.)

But when Noah heard that God still loved him and sent his Son Jesus to earth to rescue him, Noah was SO HAPPY!

AND WHEN NOAH HEARD THAT JESUS HAD DIED IN NOAH'S PLACE ON A CROSS, NOAH WAS SO THANKFUL AND LOVED JESUS EVEN MORE!

NOAH NEVER, EVER

WANTED TO BE SEPARATED FROM JESUS EVER AGAIN!

So when Noah heard that ALL
he had to do was ask Jesus to forgive him,
and come into his life,
and make his heart clean,
NOAH DIDN'T DOUBT,
HE DIDN'T STOP TO THINK ABOUT IT,
HE JUST ASKED.
THE BEST PART ABOUT FAITH
is that what we see
ISN'T PRETEND!
IT'S REAL!
So when Noah asked Jesus to come
give him new life...
Jesus REALLY came!
And Noah knew that he would
REALLY be with Jesus forever!

44

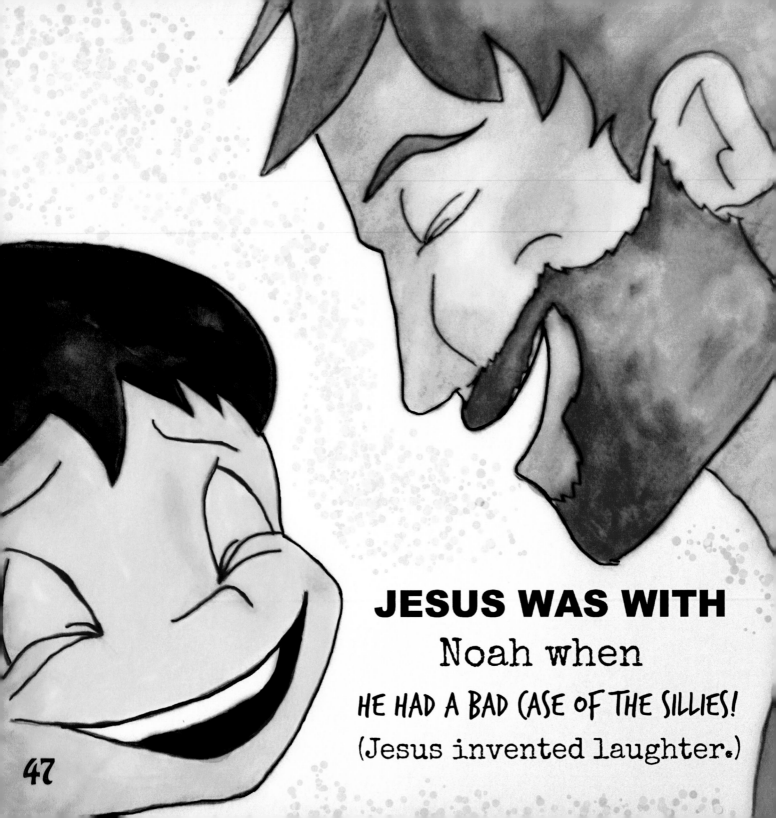

JESUS WAS WITH
Noah when
HE HAD A BAD CASE OF THE SILLIES!
(Jesus invented laughter.)

47

Noah slept safe AND SOUND since he KNEW he was wrapped tightly in JESUS' arms.

Even though Noah can't see,
he has **much better focus** than
all of us. He doesn't have as many
distractions as we do, so he is able to pay
attention to the **things that really matter...**
AND WHAT MATTERS MOST IS JESUS!

More than he wanted to be a superhero, or a
famous athlete...

Noah wanted to be close to Jesus.

**HE WANTED ALL OF JESUS THAT
HE COULD HAVE!**

He didn't want to just meet Jesus in Heaven, he
wanted to be Jesus' friend **NOW**.

And the best part is,...**Jesus says that we can
be as close to Him as we want to be!**

Anytime we reach out for Him, He **ALWAYS**
reaches back for us! ☆

When Noah heard more about Jesus' beautiful home in a place called Heaven, and how he would live in Jesus' house forever, Noah COULDN'T WAIT!!!...

And when Noah heard that Heaven was a perfect place with no more pain or problems, he knew that **HE WOULDN'T BE BLIND ANYMORE**! Jesus would open up his eyes, and he would be able to see EVERYTHING! Noah decided that the first thing he wanted to look at, was JESUS' Face!

And it was JUST like Jesus was the ONLY ONE in the room!

When Noah began using his faith vision more and more,

SOMETHING AMAZING STARTED HAPPENING!

After spending so much time with Jesus, learning about His character and listening to His Word...

NOAH STARTED TO ACT LIKE JESUS!

He was kind to his brothers
and sisters,
EVEN WHEN THEY WERE MEAN TO HIM!
He obeyed his mom and dad,
EVEN WHEN THEY ASKED HIM TO DO
THINGS THAT HE DIDN'T WANT TO DO!
He started telling everyone he
met about God's love,
AND HE WASN'T AFRAID TO DO IT!

58

Even though no one alive has ☆
seen God's face, or knows the shape of His
eyes, or the curve of His nose,
when Noah started acting like Jesus...
people could watch him and get a

GOOD IDEA OF WHAT JESUS LOOKS LIKE.

As you know, the most important part
of a person is what happens on the
INSIDE. So when Noah started to show
☆ people Jesus' heart,

THEY COULD SEE THE MOST REAL PART OF THEIR CREATOR.

Miracle of Miracles...

A boy who has never seen a sunrise, or the
colors of a rainbow,

HAS GLIMPSED THE HEART OF GOD.

A child who has never seen his own face in the
mirror, has been used to

MAKE THE INVISIBLE GOD, VISIBLE.

PUT YOUR LIFE IN
FRONT OF A MIRROR TODAY.

Examine the way you treat your family, friends, and the new people that you meet.

DOES THE WAY YOU LIVE REFLECT GOD'S HEART?
DO YOU SHOW PEOPLE WHAT JESUS LOOKS LIKE?

Noah wanted me to tell you the BEST news of ALL!

This adventure isn't JUST for Noah!!
It's for YOU too!
You don't have to be blind to live a life
filled with invisible adventures.
Jesus wants to come into YOUR life
and use YOU to show the world what He looks like.
Jesus is right here in this very room with you,
RIGHT NOW,
and is ready to take you
on an EXCITING adventure into His heart.
The only question that remains is,

"Will you say yes?"

YOU

62

Treasure Chest

Yo-Ho, me maties! I'm right PROUD of ye fer using yer noggin to make yer way to the **PRIZE**! If there's one thing Noah wants ye to know, it's that God's Word makes yer FAITH COME ALIVE! Ye can't open yer faith eyes until ye KNOW what He says and BELIEVE it, no matter what yer other eyes are tellin ye! Practice usin yer faith eyes by readin these words from the Bible and living like they are true, because they REALLY ARE!

Pg. 37

"Faith means being sure of the things we hope for and knowing that something is real even if we do not see it." Hebrews 11:1

"Here I am! I stand at the door and knock. If you hear my voice and open the door, I will come in" Revelation 3:20

"All things are worth nothing compared with the greatness of knowing Christ Jesus my Lord." Philippians 3:8b

Pg. 41

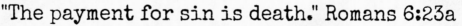

"God began by making one person, and from him came all the different people who live everywhere in the world...God wanted them to look for him and perhaps search all around for him and find him." Acts 17:26-27

"Everyone has sinned and fallen short of God's glorious standard." Romans 3:23

"The payment for sin is death." Romans 6:23a

"God loved the world so much that he gave his one and only Son so that whoever believes in him may not be lost, but have eternal life." John 3:16

"Jesus gave Himself for our sins to free us from this evil world we live in, as God the Father planned." Galatians 1:4

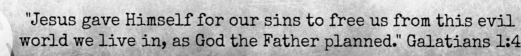

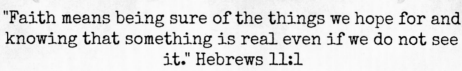

Pg. 43

"But if we confess our sins, He will forgive our sins, because we can trust God to do what is right. He will cleanse us from all the wrongs we have done." 1 John 1:9

"Anyone who calls on the Lord will be saved." Romans 10:13

Pg. 45

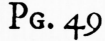

"I will be with you always, even until the end of this age." Matthew 28:19

Pg. 49

"I go to bed and sleep in peace, because, LORD, only You keep me safe." Psalm 4:8

Pg. 51

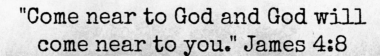

"Come near to God and God will come near to you." James 4:8

Pg. 53

"After I go and prepare a place for you, I will come back and take you to be with Me so that you may be where I am." John 14:3

"He will wipe away every tear from their eyes, and there will be no more death, sadness, crying, or pain, because all the old ways are gone." Revelation 21:4

"Now we see a dim reflection, as if we were looking into a mirror, but then we shall see clearly." 1 Corinthians 13:12a

Pg. 55

"Be careful! When you do good things, don't do them in front of people to be seen by them. If you do that, you will have no reward from your Father in Heaven." Matthew 6:6

Pg. 56

"David danced with all his might before the LORD." 2 Samuel 6:14

Pg. 57

"Whoever says that he lives in God must live as Jesus lived." 1 John 2:6

Pg. 58

"Be kind and loving to each other, and forgive each other just as God forgave you in Christ." Ephesians 4:32

"Children, obey your parents in all things, because this pleases the Lord." Colossians 3:20

"God did not give us a spirit that makes us afraid but a spirit of power and love and self-control." 2 Timothy 2:7

Pg. 59

"No one has ever seen God, but if we love each other, God lives in us, and His love is made perfect in us." 1 John 4:12

"You must love each other as I have loved you. All people will know that you are My followers if you love one another. " John 13:34b-35.....Jesus

MEET THE REAL NOAH!

Jumpin on the trampoline!

Noah worships with all his heart!

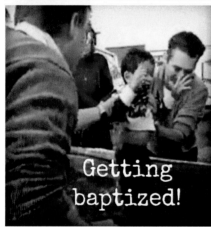

Getting baptized!

Noah and the author.

Eatin cheeseballs!

Noah swings with the author!

Noah driving!

Noah sings!

Noah and his sister at the 4th of July!

Rollerskating!

Noah the ringbearer.

Playing the piano!

THE REAL LIFE NOAH LIVES IN WEST VIRGINIA WITH HIS AMAZING PARENTS AND 11 BROTHERS AND SISTERS! (AND 3 SIBLINGS ALL GROWN UP)

Noah would LOVE to hear from you about your VERY OWN adventures! You can write to Noah by sending an email to Noahsinvisibleadventures@gmail.com. Tell him how you use the eyes of your imagination and your faith to make everyday exciting!

Noah can't wait to talk to all of you!